HIGHLIGHTS

QUEENSLAND

A Pictorial Journey

HIGHLIGHTS
QUEENSLAND

A Pictorial Journey

Brisbane

NHIL (Shaen Adey)

Cairns

Cairns

NHIL (Shaen Adey)

Above: Cape York

Left: Airlie Beach, Whitsunday Islands

Above: Palm Cove

Right: Whitsunday Islands

NHIL (Anthony Johnson)

Cairns

NHIL (Shaen Adey)

Above: Mission Beach

Right: Q1 Resort & Spa, Surfers Paradise

NHIL

Above: Mossman Gorge, Daintree National Park

Left: Townsville

Above: Trinity Beach

Right: Radical Bay, Magnetic Island

Above: Hastings Street, Noosa Heads

Right: Brisbane River

Brisbane

Courtesy of Tourism Queensland

Above: Brisbane

Left: South Bank Parklands, South Brisbane

Above: Whitehaven Beach, Whitsunday Islands

Right: Heron Island, Great Barrier Reef

26

Carnarvon Gorge National Park

NHIL (Shaen Adey)

Tamborine Mountain, Gold Coast hinterland

NHIL (Shaen Adey)

Above: Queenslander church

Left: Heron Island, Great Barrier Reef

Brisbane

Courtesy of Tourism Queensland

Above: Mungalli Falls

Right: Mulgrave River, Gordonvale

Queenslander house

Australia Zoo, Beerwah

THE REEF HOTEL CASINO

NHIL (Shaen Adey)

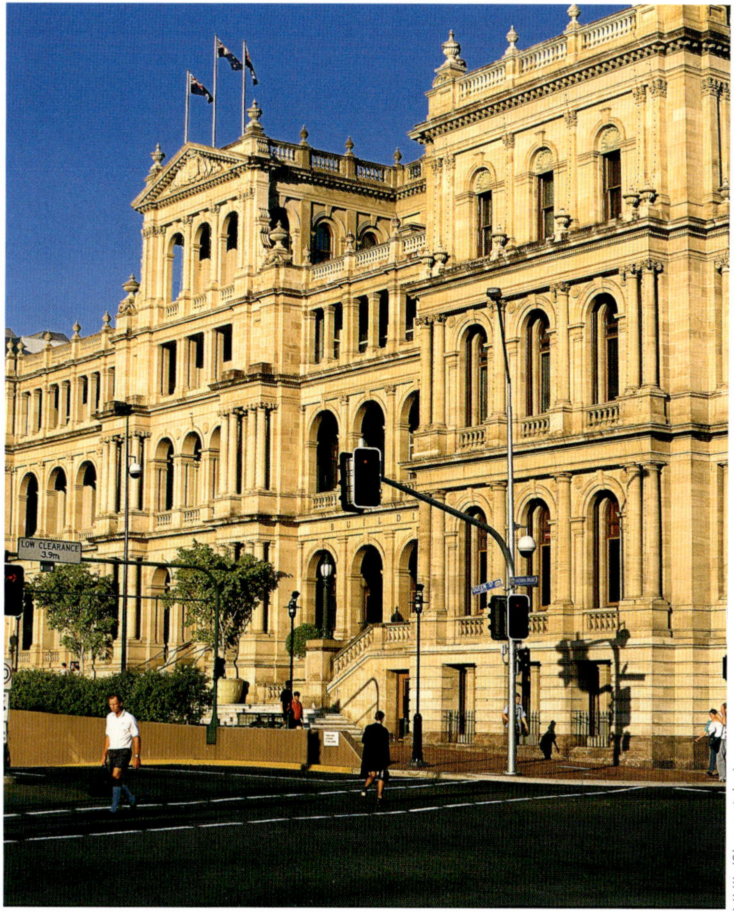

NHIL (Shaen Adey)

Above: Conrad Treasury Casino, Brisbane

Left: Reef Hotel and Casino, Townsville

Cairns Museum

NHIL (Anthony Johnson)

Cairns Pier and Marina

Brisbane

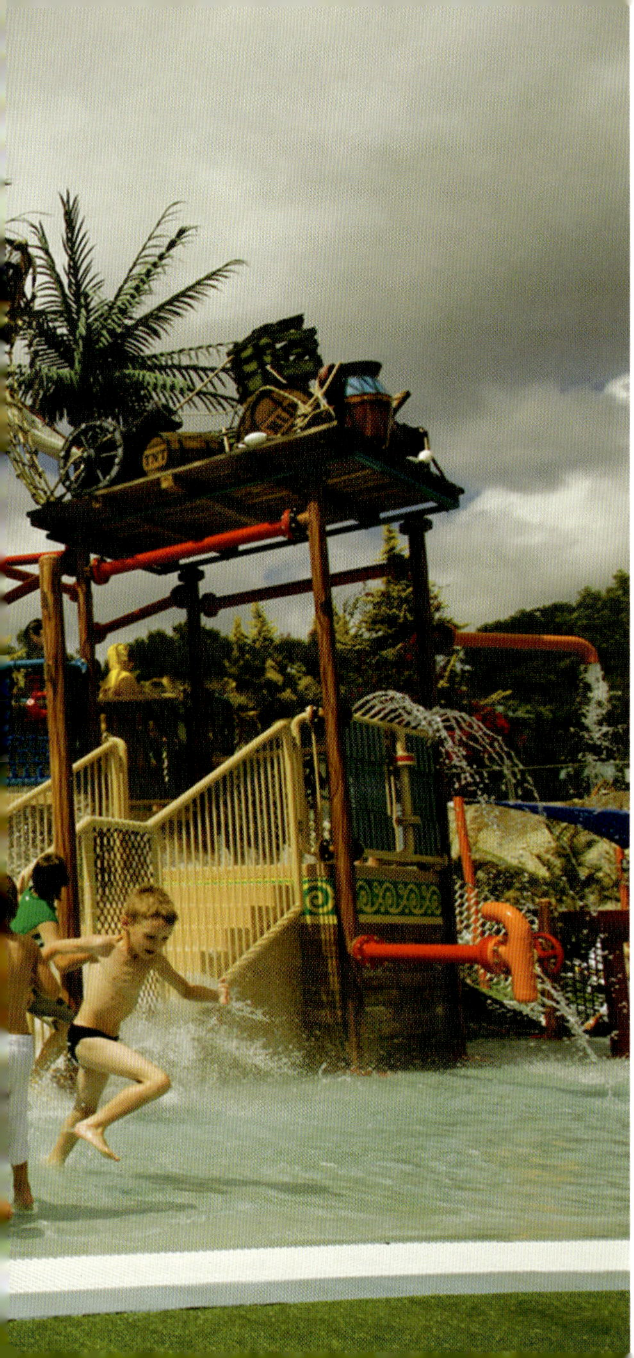

Courtesy of Sea World & Wet'n'Wild Water World

Courtesy of Sea World & Wet'n'Wild Water World

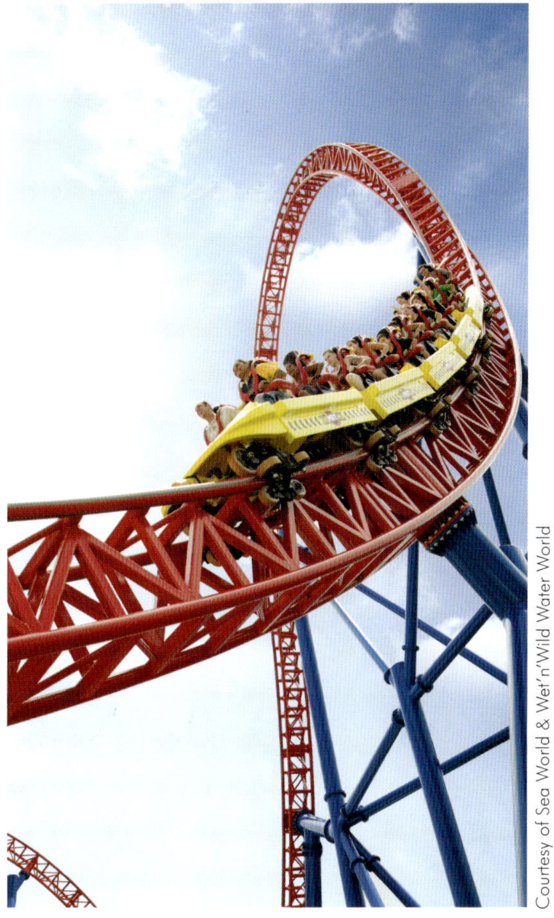

Above: Warner Bros Movie World, Gold Coast

Left: Wet'n'Wild Water World, Gold Coast

Courtesy of Sea World & Wet'n'Wild Water World

Above: Polar bear cubs at Sea World, Gold Coast

Left: Dolphins at Sea World, Gold Coast

Sea World, Gold Coast

48

Sea World, Gold Coast

Courtesy of Sea World & Wet'n'Wild Water World

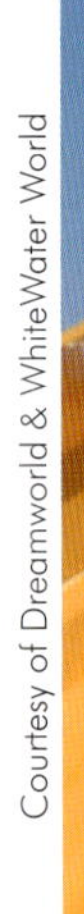

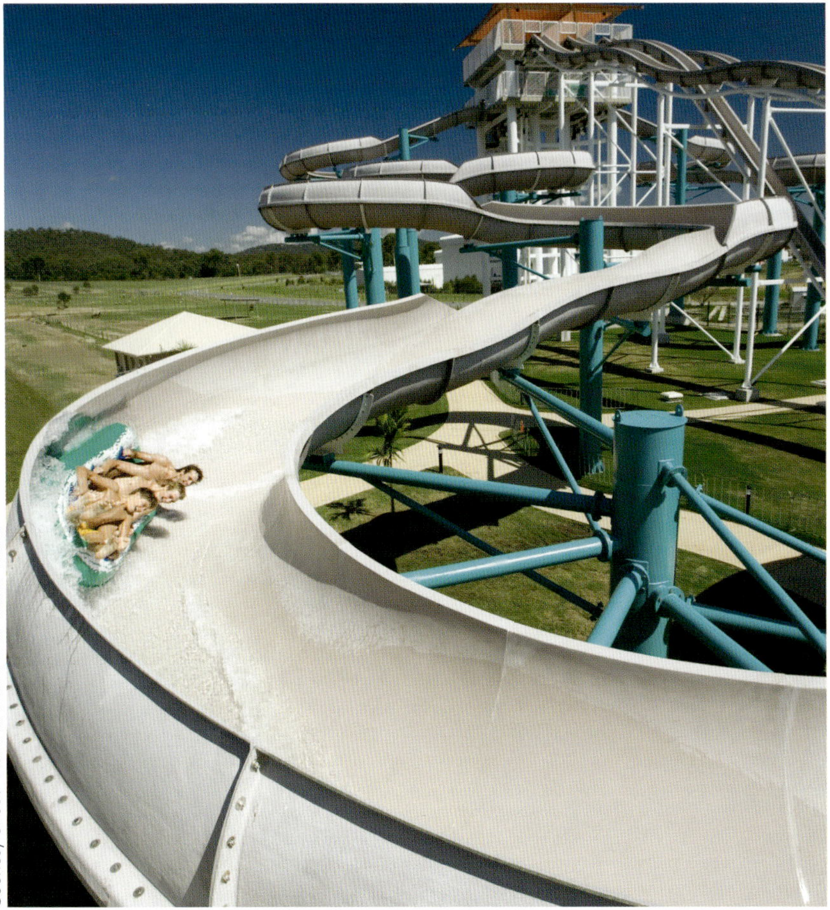

Courtesy of Dreamworld & WhiteWater World

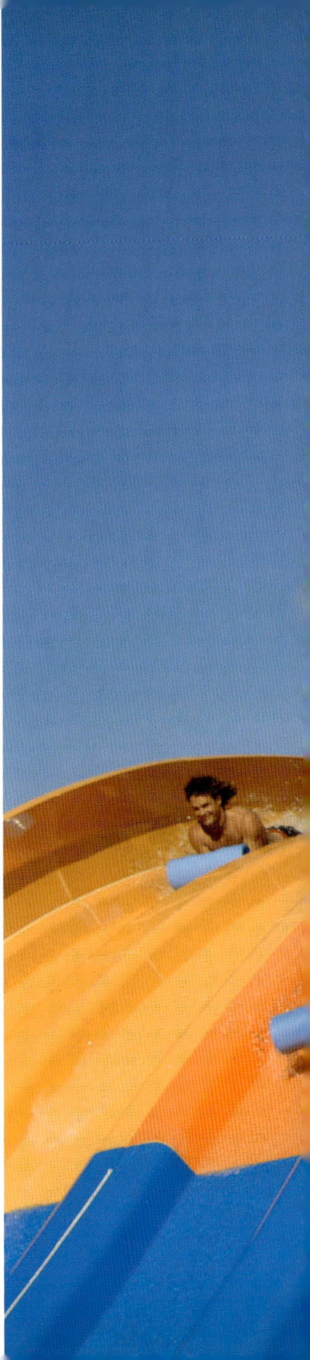

Above: Wet'n'Wild, Gold Coast

Right: WhiteWater World, Coomera

Above: Wharf Street, Maryborough, Fraser Coast

Right: Picnic Point, Toowoomba

Courtesy of Tourism Queensland

Southport, Gold Coast

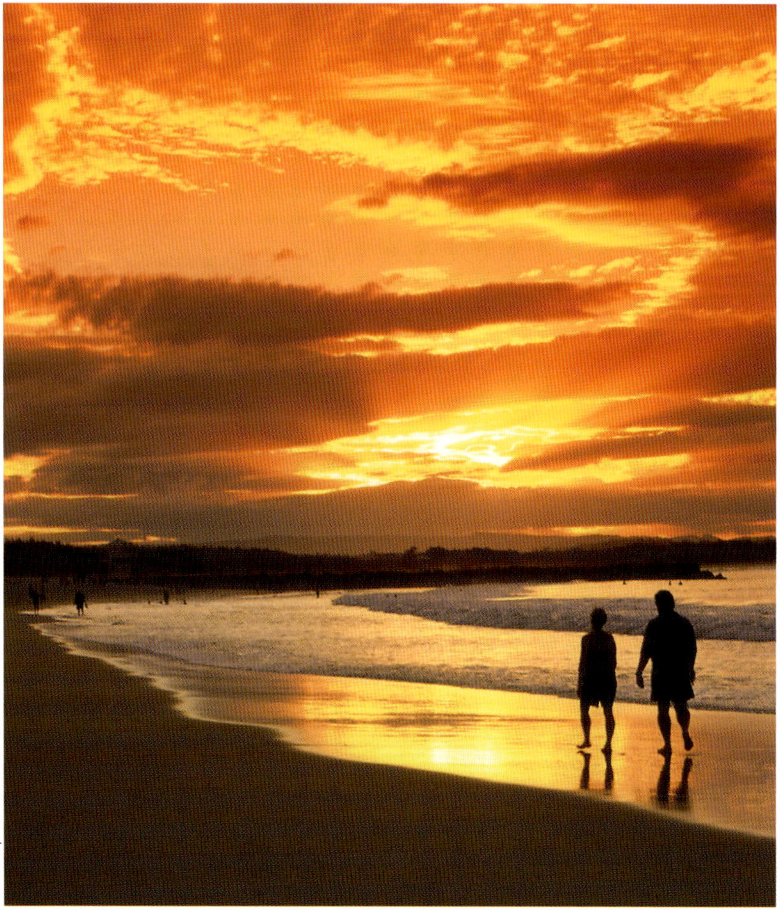

Courtesy of Tourism Queensland

Courtesy of Tourism Queensland

Above: Noosa Heads, Sunshine Coast

Right: Noosa National Park, Sunshine Coast

Courtesy of Tourism Queensland

Above: Hinchinbrook Island, near Townsville

Left: Great Barrier Reef

Above: Main Beach, Noosa, Sunshine Coast

Right: Cape Hillsborough National Park, Mackay

Courtesy of Tourism Queensland

Lizard Island, Great Barrier Reef

Courtesy of Tourism Queensland

Courtesy of Tourism Queensland

Above: Great Barrier Reef

Left: Horseshoe Bay, Magnetic Island

The Spit, Main Beach, Gold Coast

Hamilton Island, Whitsunday Islands

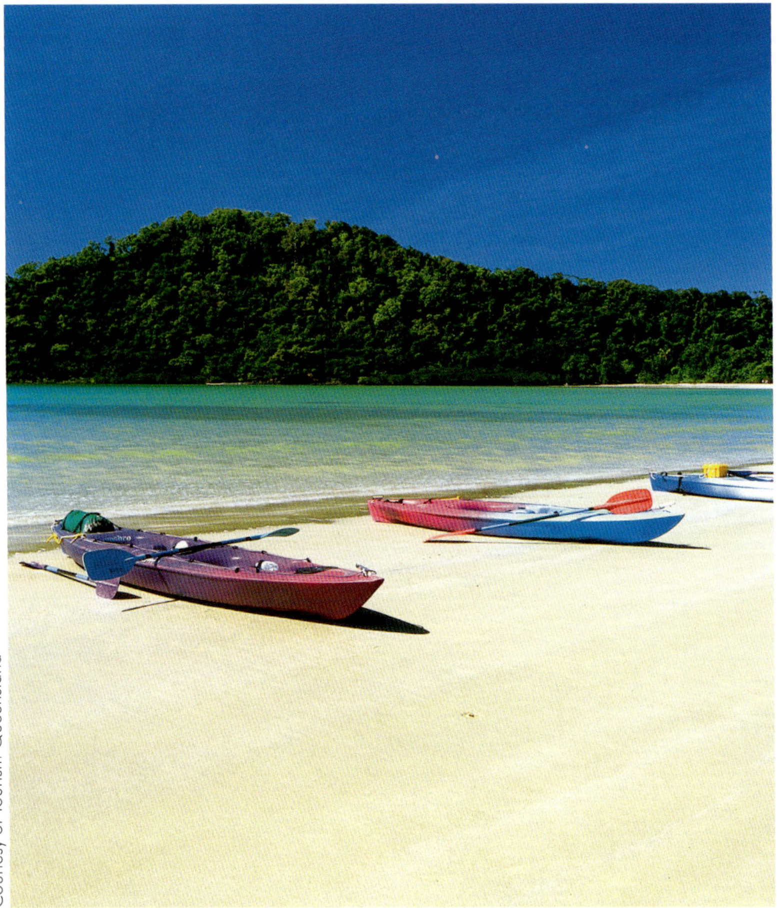

Courtesy of Tourism Queensland

Courtesy of Tourism Queensland

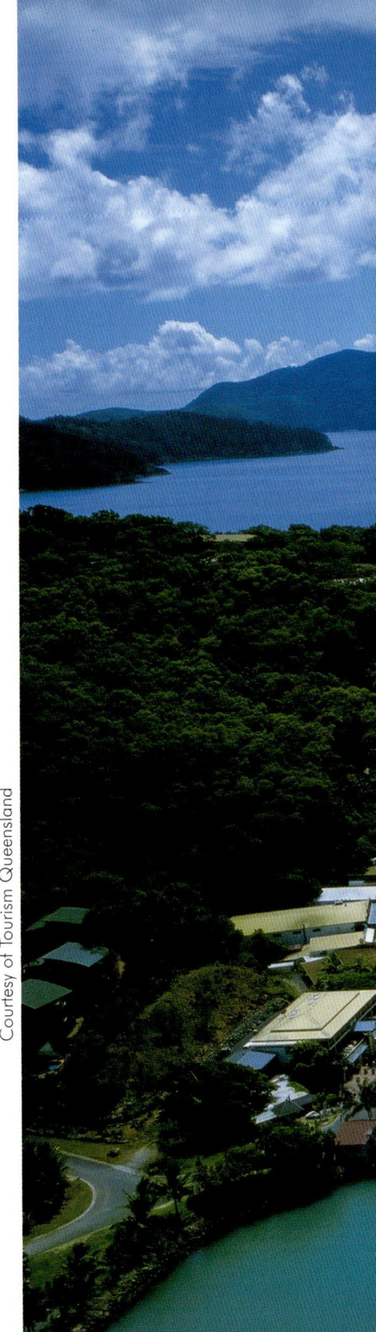

Above: Cape Tribulation

Right: Hamilton Island, Whitsunday Islands

Courtesy of Tourism Queensland

Above: Four Mile Beach, Port Douglas

Left: Road to Port Douglas, Cairns

Above: Normanton, Gulf of Carpentaria

Right: Bundaberg

The Strand, Townsville

Courtesy of Tourism Queensland

Above: Mardja Boardwalk, Daintree National Park

Right: Girraween National Park, Southern Downs region

Clyde Hotel, Calliope Historical Village, near Gladstone

Courtesy of Tourism Queensland

Above: Longreach

Left: Blackdown Tableland National Park

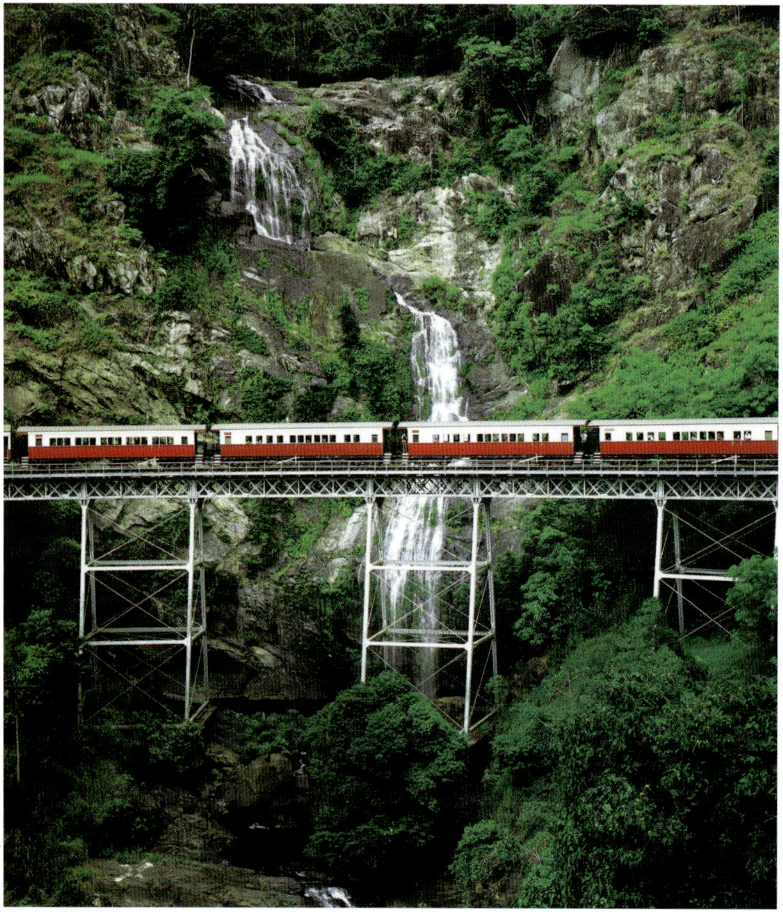

Courtesy of Tourism Queensland

Courtesy of Tourism Queensland

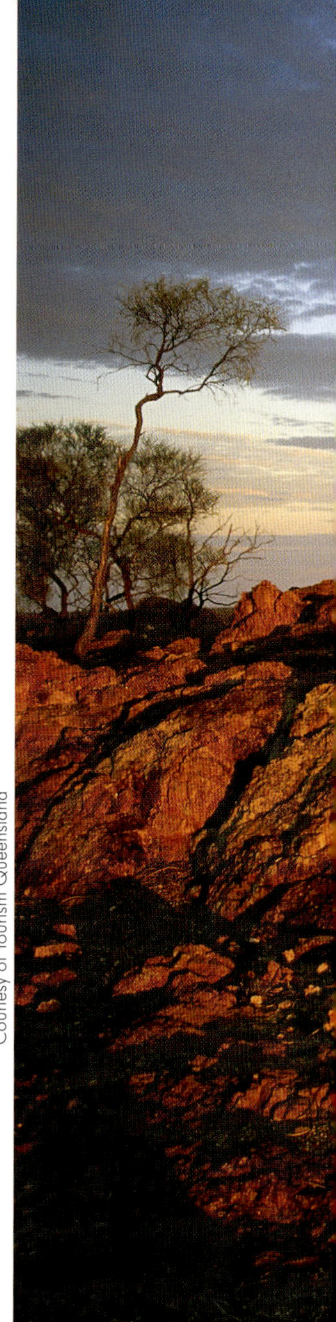

Above: Kuranda Scenic Rail and Stoney Creek Falls, Kuranda

Right: Mayfield Station, Windorah

Roma

Courtesy of Tourism Queensland

Above: Clifton

Right: Hayman Island, Whitsunday Islands

Courtesy of Tourism Queensland

Above: Jericho

Left: Birdsville

Radical Bay, Magnetic Island

Above: Botanical Gardens

Right: Fitzroy River, Rockhampton, near Capricorn

92

Castle Rock overlooking Gulf Savannah, near Forsayth

Courtesy of Tourism Queensland

First published in Australia in 2007 by
New Holland Publishers (Australia) Pty Ltd
Sydney • Auckland • London • Cape Town

1/66 Gibbes Street Chatswood NSW 2067 Australia
218 Lake Road Northcote Auckland New Zealand
86 Edgware Road London W2 2EA United Kingdom
80 McKenzie Street Cape Town 8001 South Africa

Picture Credits

Q1 Resort & Spa: cover
Tourism Queensland: back cover bottom left, back cover centre, back cover centre right
NHIL (Shaen Adey): back cover centre left; title; pp. 1–2
NHIL: back cover top

National Library of Australia Cataloguing-in-Publication Data:

Highlights: Queensland.

ISBN 9781741106114 (hbk.).

1. Queensland - Pictorial works. 2. Australia - Pictorial
works. I. Hills, Sally. (Series : Highlight series).

919.43

Publisher: Fiona Schultz
Project Editor: Sally Hills
Designer: Hayley Norman
Production Manager: Linda Bottari
Printer: SNP Leefung

10 9 8 7 6 5 4 3 2 1